ant farm

ant farm

and
other
desperate
situations

simon rich

RANDOM HOUSE TRADE PAPERBACKS

NEW YORK

A Random House Trade Paperback Original

Published in the United States by Random House Trade Paperbacks, an imprint of The Random House Publishing Group, a division of Random House, Inc., New York.

RANDOM HOUSE TRADE PAPERBACKS and colophon are trademarks of Random House, Inc.

Approximately half of the pieces in this work were originally published in *The Harvard Lampoon* from 2003 to 2006.

ISBN 978-1-4000-6563-9

LIBRARY OF CONGRESS CATALOGING-IN-PUBLICATION DATA

Rich, Simon.
Ant farm : and other desperate situations / Simon Rich.
p.   cm.
ISBN-13: 978-1-4000-6588-2
1. American wit and humor. I. Title.
PN6165.R53 2007
818'.602—dc22   2006051043

Printed in the United States of America

www.atrandom.com

6897

Book design by Carole Lowenstein

For my mom

contents

V

Then Abraham tied Isaac up and laid him on the altar
over the wood. And Abraham took the knife and lifted it up
to kill his son as a sacrifice to the LORD.
At that moment the angel of the LORD shouted to him
from heaven, "Abraham! Lay down the knife." . . .
Then they returned to Beersheba.
—GENESIS 22

the ride back to beersheba

How about some ice cream, Isaac? No? Are you sure? I'll tell you what, I'll get us some ice cream. Want some ice cream? I'll get us some ice cream.

Wow, there is nothing like camping! Cooking your own lamb, building your own pyre . . . and no women! Just a couple of guys in the woods, lighting fires, doing stuff, and keeping it between themselves! Speaking of which, did you ever notice how your mother sometimes gets ideas? I mean, she raised you and I love her, but she's a very nervous person. All I'm saying is sometimes it's all right not to tell her about certain things. Like *guy* things.

Wow, I just noticed that you have *huge* muscles! You're really getting strong! When did you get so big and strong? Soon you'll be a real strong guy!

Let me explain something to you. Sometimes, grown-ups have to do grown-up stuff that children don't understand. I think there's an ice cream place coming up. Like, what happened on top of the mountain? Do you remember? Of course you . . . of course. Anyway, that was a thing for grown-ups.

How about some Rocky Road? Chocolate? I'd get you some strawberry, but hey, your name's Isaac, not Isaac-Marie—am I right? Ha! Seriously, though, if you want strawberry I'll get it for you. I'll get you whatever you want.

So, anyway, let's rehearse. I'll be your mother. "Isaac, how was your trip to the mountain?" Okay, then you would say something like "Pretty normal." That's not too hard, right?

We're almost home. Listen, I probably shouldn't be telling you this, but your mother is very sick. She's sick, Isaac. And the slightest shock might kill her. Hey, there she is, waving at us! *Hi, Sarah, we're back!* Put a couple lambs on the spit—you've got a couple hungry *lumber-jacks* on your hands! Ha, ha! She's very ill, Isaac. Very ill. Wow! . . . *Camping.*

a conversation
at the grown-ups' table
as imagined at the kids' table

MOM: Pass the wine, please. I want to become crazy.

DAD: Okay.

GRANDMOTHER: Did you see the politics? It made me angry.

DAD: Me too. When it was over, I had sex.

UNCLE: I'm having sex right now.

DAD: We all are.

MOM: Let's talk about which kid I like the best.

DAD: (laughing) You know, but you won't tell.

MOM: If they ask me again, I might tell.

FRIEND FROM WORK: Hey, guess what? My voice is pretty loud!

DAD: (laughing) There are actual monsters in the world, but when my kids ask I pretend like there aren't.

MOM: I'm angry! I'm angry all of a sudden!

DAD: I'm angry too! We're angry at each other!

MOM: Now everything is fine.

DAD: We just saw the PG-13 movie. It was so good.

MOM: There was a big sex.

FRIEND FROM WORK: I am the loudest! I am the loudest!

(Everybody laughs.)

MOM: I had a lot of wine, and now I'm crazy!

GRANDFATHER: Hey, do you guys know what God looks like?

ALL: Yes.

GRANDFATHER: Don't tell the kids.

second grade realization

—Jake, come over here for a second. I need to talk to you about something.

—What's up?

—This is going to sound a little crazy. Oh well . . . here goes. Do you remember when we were on the school bus last week and Ms. Higgins taught us that new game?

—You mean the Silent Game? Yeah, I remember. It was pretty cool of her to let us play games on the bus, huh?

—Well, yeah, that's what I thought at first. But then I started thinking about it. And now I'm not so sure.

—What do you mean?

—Well, just think about it. The Silent Game isn't *actually* fun. We don't do anything—we just kind of sit there. And nobody ever wins. It's always a tie.

—What are you saying?

—I don't think it's a real game. I think she just made it up to get us to be quiet.

—Oh my God. I think you're right.

—I can't believe we fell for it. We were silent for almost twenty minutes!

—We have to tell the class!

—What's the point? They'd never believe us.

—What about all the other games she taught us? The Politeness Game . . . the Respect Game . . . the Clean Up the Tables Game . . .

—What about them?

—Those might be fake too.

—Whoa. You just blew my mind.

—This has got to be the craziest day of my life.

a day at
UNICEF headquarters
as i imagined it in third grade

[UNICEF sits on a throne. He is wearing a cape and holding a scepter. A servant enters, on his knees.]

UNICEF: Halloween is fast approaching! Have the third graders been given their little orange boxes?

SERVANT: Yes, your majesty!

UNICEF: Perfect. Did you tell them what the money was for?

SERVANT: No, sir, of course not! We just gave them the boxes and told them to collect for UNICEF. We said it was for "a good cause," but we didn't get any more specific than that.

UNICEF: Ha ha ha! Those fools! Soon I will have all the money in the world. For I am UNICEF, *evil king of Halloween!*

SERVANT: Sir . . . don't you think you've stolen enough

from the children? Maybe you should let them keep the money this year?

UNICEF: Never! The children shall toil forever to serve my greed!

[UNICEF tears open a little orange box and rubs the coins all over his fat stomach.]

UNICEF: Yes! Oh, yes!

SERVANT: Wait—your majesty! Look at this! Our records indicate that there's a kid out there—Simon—who's planning to *keep* his UNICEF money this year.

UNICEF: What?!? But what about my evil plans? I was going to give that money to the Russians so they could build a bomb!

SERVANT: I guess there's still one hero left in this world.

UNICEF: Noooo!

[Runs out of castle, sobbing.]

SERVANT: Thank God Simon is keeping his UNICEF money.

SECOND SERVANT: Yes, it's good that he's keeping the money.

THIRD SERVANT: I agree. Simon is doing a good thing by keeping the money from the UNICEF box.

SERVANT: Then we're all in agreement. Simon should keep the money.

---

i still remember the day
i got my first calculator

TEACHER: All right, children, welcome to fourth grade math. Everybody take a calculator out of the bin.

ME: What are these?

TEACHER: From now on we'll be using calculators.

ME: What do these things do?

TEACHER: Simple operations, like multiplication and division.

ME: You mean this device just . . . does them? By itself?

TEACHER: Yes. You enter in the problem and press equal.

ME: You . . . you knew about this machine all along, didn't you? This whole time, while we were going through this . . . this *charade* with the pencils and the line paper and *the stupid multiplication tables!* . . . I'm sorry for shouting . . . It's just . . . I'm a little blown away.

TEACHER: Okay, everyone, today we're going to go over some word problems.

ME: What the hell else do you have back there? A magical pen that writes book reports by itself? Some kind of automatic social studies worksheet that . . . that fills itself out? What the hell is going on?

TEACHER: If a farmer farms five acres of land a day—

ME: So that's it, then. The past three years have been a total farce. All this time I've been thinking, "Well, this is pretty hard and frustrating but I guess these are useful skills to have." Meanwhile, there was a whole bin of these things in your desk. We could have jumped straight to graphing. Unless, of course, there's some kind of graphing calculator!

TEACHER: There is. You get one in ninth grade.

ME: Is this . . . Am I on TV? Is this a prank show?

TEACHER: No.

playing nice

Dear fourth grade parents,

In order to make sure no child gets hurt this year, the PTA has agreed to the following guidelines for birthday parties:

1. If a child invites more than half of the class, he must invite the entire class, including Ivan.

2. If a child only wants to invite a few best friends but Ivan hears that there's a party, that child must invite Ivan and pretend that the party is for Ivan.

3. If Ivan is at a party and he starts to have one of his fits, everyone else at the party (including parents) must pretend to have fits also so Ivan doesn't feel that he's the only one having a fit. When Ivan runs out of steam, nobody should talk about what just happened.

4. If Ivan demands that a child invite him to a party, that child must invite Ivan to a party even if it's not that child's birthday and that child doesn't have any party planned. The next day, at the party, everybody should pretend that it actually *is* that child's birthday and Ivan was right about everything.

5. If Ivan figures out somehow that the other children have been faking their fits, the children must be taken out of school until Ivan has one of his major breakdowns and loses his recent memory.

6. No matter whose party it is, Ivan always blows out the candles and opens all the presents.

Thank you,
Mrs. Billings

our thoughts are with you

Dear Mrs. Matthews,

I am writing to express my deepest sympathies. I shared your last note with Caleb's classmates and they made a card (which I have enclosed). Ten funerals in three weeks is a lot to ask of any child, let alone a child like Caleb, who has already suffered so many family deaths this month. At first, as humiliating as it is to admit, I thought your son had forged the notes. But denial quickly gave way to grief. I understand he has another funeral to attend on Wednesday and that it will last until Friday. Please let him know that he can take as much time off as he needs. I would volunteer to drop off Caleb's home-work myself, but I understand that your house recently exploded. Of all the tragedies that have befallen your family, this one saddened me the most. For a house to suddenly explode, without warning, destroying a child's backpack and books, is very upsetting, particularly in the midst of your High Voodoo Holidays.

I was also deeply saddened to learn that your son had suffered brain damage and could no longer complete his social studies assignments. To be hit with such a misfortune, on top of Tourette's, is a blow to any child's self-esteem, especially when that child is retarded.

Incidentally, I understand that Caleb has recently taken on some serious community service projects. I totally understand Caleb's devotion to the blind, particularly in light of his own blindness. But I'm worried that his extracurricular activities might interfere with his schoolwork, especially on top of the pressures of his upcoming Voodoo Bar Mitzvah. Of course, it's your decision.

I would also like to take this opportunity to congratulate you on your son's recent achievement! To be named an FBI super-spy at such a young age is an amazing accomplishment, particularly for a child who suffers from so many varied forms of brain damage. He hasn't told me much about his mission, but from what I gather it sounds like an incredible opportunity. I'm going to miss his presence in the classroom next year, but it would be selfish of me to stand in his way. Caleb's country needs him more than I do. He belongs in Russia.

Rest assured: I haven't told anyone about Caleb's mission, not even the principal. I am honored that Caleb felt he could trust me with top secret information, and I would *never* betray that trust.

Godspeed,
Mr. Marks

math problems

Please show your work.

1. A name-brand bottle of rum costs $12.95. The generic brand sells for $7.50. If a math teacher buys 4 bottles of generic rum each week, how much does he save each month? How much does he save each year? How much money does the teacher save over the course of 11 years?

2. A math teacher's new apartment is approximately 12 ft. long and 5 ft. wide, and the bathroom takes up 50% of the apartment. A normal human-size bed is 6 ft. × 3 ft. Does the math teacher have enough room for a standard bed? Or will he have to sleep in some kind of dog bed?

3. By order of the high courts, a math teacher must keep 1,000 ft. away from his ex-wife at all times. Say, theoretically, she lives on 63rd and York, exactly halfway between the math teacher's apartment and his school. How far out of his way does the teacher have to walk every morning just to keep from getting arrested?

4. After 11 years of service, a math teacher receives an $80 gift certificate to Shaw's Gas in lieu of a raise. How much of that money will be left after taxes? Express in bottles of rum.

5. A math teacher is frightened 95% of the time. How many hours a day is he frightened? What is he so afraid of?

＿

:(

i used 2 B a typical teenage girl, gossiping with my gal friends on the weekends (I luv U guys!) throwing slumber parties (zzzzzzz!) That was B4 i contracted hepatitis C.

Sometimes i ask myself, "Y?˙ Y has the lord 4saken me? R U there God? Have U 4gotten me?" i'm trying 2 B positive, but it's hard when U know that your death is a 4gone conclusion. It's only a matter of time B4 my D4med liver ceases 2 function 4ever.

My innards R swarming w/2morous growths & the pain is excruci8ing. i no longer have any will 2 live. 2morrow i'll B sed8ed 4 the oper8ion. Secretly, i hope i don't come 2.

i've decided 2 stop praying. Y should I? i h8 god. He sh@ on me & i h8 him.

All i can do now is w8 4 death.

:(

if life were like middle school

JUDGE: In all my years on the bench, I have never seen a more despicable criminal. You robbed, assaulted, and tortured the victim simply for the thrill of it. Do you have anything to say in your defense before I sentence you?

CRIMINAL: Nope.

JUDGE: In that case, I hereby sentence you to forty years in a maximum security prison. I also sentence the victim to forty years in prison.

VICTIM: Wait—*what*? That doesn't make any sense! *He* attacked *me*!

JUDGE: I don't care who started it.

pen pal

In seventh grade, everyone in my class was assigned a foreign pen pal. Mine was from Bulgaria, and his name was Bojidar. We exchanged letters once a month, and at the end of the year we wrote reports about each other's countries based on what we had learned. Here is his report:

LIFE IN THE USA
By Bojidar

Of all the boys in the United States, Simon is the most popular. Simon is especially very popular with the girls at his school. I am very lucky that I was assigned the pen pal Simon, because it turns out that he is a very important American!

To the American girls, Simon is like a matador. They

carry around in their pockets pictures of his face, and they trade the pictures to each other like they are currency. Rebecca, the most beautiful girl in America, wants to be his girlfriend but she does not say anything to him about it because she is afraid he will say no. The girls are impressed with Simon because (1) he does very well at all the videogames, and (2) he knows all the facts about the planets in outer space.

The cool things to wear in America are sweatpants, hand-me-down T-shirts, and big braces on your mouth and head. Another cool thing is to wear Velcro shoes. Here is a photograph of my pen pal. The average height for a thirteen-year-old boy in the United States is four feet five inches tall. So although he is small by the Bulgarian standard, in the United States, Simon is a boy of average size.

In the United States, a normal thing for boys is to go to a speech doctor every day after school to learn how to make the *l, s, r,* and *t* sounds. This is not something that is weird in the United States.

In the United States, a cool thing is to listen to songs from the Disney movies, such as *Aladdin, Small Mermaid,* and *Beauty and Beast.* Here is an example about that: One time my pen pal was listening to a tape of Disney songs on a Walkman machine, and Trevor, the leader of the lacrosse team, opened the machine and saw that the tape inside was *Small Mermaid*. There were a lot of girls from the school standing near them also. When Trevor looked at the tape, he said something like "That is a normal thing for a boy to be listening to, you are a cool guy." Then Trevor and the girls came over to Simon's house and they all listened to the Disney songs together and became friends. That is how things work in America.

a fantasy i had
in seventh grade

Dear seventh graders,

Congratulations to all of the students who passed the Presidential Fitness Test! In three weeks, you will be engaged in warfare with the enemies of the United States.

I'd like to give special kudos to football co-captains Lance and Trevor, who both scored above the 90th percentile. You'll be going directly to the front lines.

Unfortunately, those of you who scored beneath the 35th percentile will not be allowed to participate in this war. You will, however, get to help out with strategizing—i.e., deciding which soldiers go on the most dangerous missions.

Also, I have been informed that while some of you lack athletic ability, you are very talented at computer simulation games. I cannot tell you how highly these skills are prized in today's modern army. Next week, we will be having a Presidential Videogame Fitness Test. Anyone who scores higher than 7,000 points on CrystalQuest will be given control of the entire Western Front. Anyone who scores higher than 8,000 points will become President.

Good luck to you all,

The President

inside the cartridge

—How many dead?

—Fifty.

—Christ. Exactly the same as yesterday. How's morale?

—Terrible. It's like we're not even trying out there. We don't stand a chance against . . . well . . . you know.

—(shuddering) He-Who-Is-Dressed-Differently.

—He's immortal, and I'll swear to that. Today he stopped in midstride and began to punch the air. Five of our brothers walked directly into his moving fist. One by one, they fell to the ground and vanished.

—There is no God.

—Every day he defeats us in the exact same sequence, using the exact same maneuvers.

—And that music. It never stops!

—The same sixteen notes, over and over again, droning and endless, piercing through the darkened void. (hushed) Sometimes he brings a companion to help him with his murders.

—Their blows hurt us but not each other!

—It is as if God has chosen us alone for misery.

—(sobbing) Why does he rush through our town so quickly?

—I believe he's going for a record of some kind. It has to do with points.

—Sweet Lord!

—It's not enough for him to simply take our lives. He must also take our honor.

—You would think by now he would have grown tired of this battle. Surely the challenge is gone!

—And yet the genocide continues.

—Was it always like this, brother?

—I do not know.

(Time pauses without warning for three and a half minutes, then resumes seamlessly.)

—Hold me, brother, I'm frightened!

—(punches him in the face) I'm sorry. That seems to be the only action I'm capable of.

—I only have two hits left.

THE END

rebellion

Unfortunately, I started rebelling against my parents at around the same time I developed body odor.

—Son, I strongly suggest that you start wearing deodorant.

—Fuck you, Dad. I've got bigger plans.

—Please, son, I'm not the only one who feels strongly about this. Your teachers sent me a letter by messenger. It was signed by some of your classmates.

—Give the Man whatever he wants, right, Dad? Always obey the Man. That's your great philosophy of life.

—Yes, that's fine, son. Listen. It's really bad. The smell is really bad.

—Hey, Dad, guess what? I'm not going to synagogue anymore.

—Okay . . . Please, son, I bought you these different kinds of deodorant. If you don't like any of them, I'll go back to the store and buy you more kinds. Hey, here's a cool one. It's for athletes.

—I'm moving out! I'm going to live under the overpass! Some of those people fought in *wars*, Dad. You didn't fight in any wars.

—Okay, that's . . . All that's fine. Please put this on, son. You . . . you carry my name.

what goes through my mind when i'm home alone (from my mom's perspective)

Hmm, Mom left me home alone. Better go through the medicine cabinet and drink all the medicine for no reason. Wait, what's this? A note telling me not to "drink any medicines"? Thank God! I was about to do that. I was about to drink all the medicines and kill myself because I'm retarded.

Well, I better use the stove and then not turn it off. That way, I'll burn down the house and kill myself. Wait a minute. There's a note that says I should "turn off the stove after using it." Jesus Christ, that never would have occurred to me! Mom saved my life again, twice in one night.

Well, better throw things out the window, something I haven't done since I was seven. I'm fifteen years old, but I haven't matured at all. I still need to be reminded constantly about how to get through the day. What? A note? Guess I shouldn't "throw objects out the window" after all. There go my big plans.

Ah . . . dinnertime. There's a Tupperware container full of pasta in the fridge, but it's cold! How will I ever heat it up? I guess I'll just starve and die because I'm not competent enough to warm pasta. Whoa! A note telling me to put the container in the microwave and press EASY MINUTE! Thanks, note! You saved my life.

I hope that when my mom comes home she asks me some very specific, humiliating questions about my changing body.

i can only think of two scenarios where high school math would come in handy

I

MURDERER: I'm a crazy person. Do this trigonometry problem or I'll murder you.

ME: Can I use a graphing calculator?

MURDERER: Yes, of course. Oh—and here's a list of necessary formulas.

ME: Great, thanks. Okay, let's see . . . $\sin2x = 2\cos x\sin x$?

MURDERER: That's correct. You're free to go.

2

OLD RICH MAN: Hello, everyone. I've gone completely insane. Whoever solves this trigonometry problem fastest gets all of the money in my will.

ME: Can we use graphing calculators?

OLD RICH MAN: Yes—and the necessary formulas are on the second page.

ME: Cool. Is it $t = 50$?

OLD RICH MAN: I need it expressed to me in radians.

ME: $t = 0.28$?

OLD RICH MAN: Congratulations, here is all my money.

slumber party

SEYMOUR: What do you guys want to do?

ZACH: Let's find your dad's liquor and drink it!

SEYMOUR: Cool! The only thing is: I don't know where the old man keeps his booze.

DAN: Well, let's split up and look for it! There are *six* of us. One of us is bound to find it.

SEYMOUR: Awesome, let's do it!

(Five minutes later.)

ZACH: I found it! It was in the first place I looked!

DAN: Really? I found some too.

MIKE: Me too. Look.

KEVIN: I . . . I also found some alcohol.

SEYMOUR: Everyone found alcohol? I don't understand. Where did you guys look?

ZACH: Under your dad's bed.

DAN: In your dad's medicine cabinet.

JOSH: Behind your dad's toilet.

KEVIN: A few different closets. And in your little sister's room . . . behind her community service trophies.

JAKE: I found a moonshine still in the basement. It looked pretty advanced. There were bags of barley and pressurized tanks. And there was some kind of silver tasting cup, hanging from a hook.

SEYMOUR: I can't believe this. I think I have to be alone for a while.

BRENT: (running in) Hey, Seymour! Guys! Guess what, I found the booze! You'll never guess where it was—in the attic inside an old box marked "Memories."

SEYMOUR: . . .

BRENT: There was a lot up there.

role playing

TEACHER: All right, class, today we're going to be learning about the political landscape that led to the Civil War. Let's start with a little role-playing exercise. First we need someone to play the part of a Southern slave owner. Okay, let's say . . . Seymour.

SEYMOUR: What?

TEACHER: Great. Now we need someone to play a Northern abolitionist. Raise your hand if you want to volunteer. Okay—I guess that's everybody else. Let's begin.

SOPHIE: How many innocent people must die to satisfy your greed, Seymour?

KAREN: You're a monster, Seymour. (crying) A *monster*.

SEYMOUR: What's happening? I'm against slavery— I swear!

TEACHER: I don't think that's something a slave owner

would say, Seymour. Remember, you're being graded on this.

SEYMOUR: Um . . . then, I guess . . . slavery . . . is good?

TEACHER: Of all the villains in the history of this nation, you, Seymour, are by far the most terrifying. I can't even look you in the face. You literally make my skin crawl.

SEYMOUR: I thought you said it was a role-playing exercise?

TEACHER: I'm also doing the exercise. I'm an abolitionist.

sex ed

MR. BENDER: Okay class, now it's time to read one of your anonymous sex questions out loud. Here's one . . .

JONATHAN: Hey, Seymour, did you write that one? That looks like your handwriting.

SEYMOUR: Mr. Bender! Don't read it!

MR. BENDER: Please, no talking. It's very important that I answer this question. Whoever asked it is obviously incredibly confused about sex. These are not normal concerns. Not even close.

SETH: Hey, I bet that's Seymour's question. It's written in blue ink like all his homework assignments.

SEYMOUR: Oh, no!

MR. BENDER: Okay, let's see . . . it's a seven-part question. The first part is about testicles.

SEYMOUR: Oh my God!

MR. BENDER: Quiet, class. We have to be fair to the boy who wrote this, even if we find his sexual desires morally reprehensible.

JONATHAN: Hey, I think that's Seymour's stationery. I can tell because of the watermark.

MR. BENDER: All right. I'm going to read the question now. But I have to warn you: It's pretty hard to take. If you feel like screaming, that's understandable. I'm probably going to do some screaming myself. It's *that* extreme.

(Bell rings.)

SEYMOUR: That's the bell! Class dismissed!

MR. BENDER: Stay in your seats, everyone. If I don't answer this student's question and he continues to masturbate in the aberrant fashion he describes in part 3, he could permanently damage his body. Okay . . . here it goes . . . Jesus Christ, I can't read this out loud, it's too humiliating. Can I have a volunteer?

SEYMOUR: I'll read it!

MR. BENDER: Here you go.

SEYMOUR: Great! Um . . . okay . . . it says . . . What do you do if you are a . . . normal boy . . . with no really weird things.

ouija board

Oh, thank God ... Five young conjurers are trying to communicate with me. Now I can finally reveal the identity of my killer!

Is there a spirit present?

Yes!

(Giggling.)

Girls, listen to me. My name is Craig Swieskowski. I was murdered by a man named Bruce Kobza.

Does Trevor like Janet?

What? How should I know? Listen, Bruce Kobza poisoned me to death! There's a video recording of the murder in a locked briefcase in his apartment. You need to break into his bedroom, unlock the briefcase and show the tape to the police!

Y ... E ... S! (Hysterical laughter.) Trevor likes you, Janet!

Okay . . . that's . . . that's fine. I'm glad we got that out of
our system. But now it's time to get serious. We might not
have another chance to talk like this. I need you girls to
go to Mt. Sinai Cemetery and dig up my body. Do an au-
topsy. You'll find—

Who likes Sophie?

Jesus, it's like you're not even listening to me! Bruce
Kobza murdered me! (sighing) Okay . . . fine, I'll try to
use the damn board. B . . .

B!

R . . .

R! Hey, he's spelling out Brian Pasternak! Brian Paster-
nak likes Sophie!

No!

Spirit? Are we pretty? Or . . . do we need to lose a little
bit of weight?

You don't need to lose any weight. . . . You should all be
thankful you're alive and healthy.

L-O-S-E W-E-I-G-H-T. Guess we'll have to keep dieting,
huh?

What? That's not what I said at all! (*Sighs.*) It doesn't
matter.

my mom's all-time top five greatest boyfriends

By Milo Farber, age 11

5. JARED MILLER

This guy was awesome! He's by far the strongest, biggest dude I've ever met. But that's not all—he also plays for the Fort Wayne Warriors, my favorite minor-league hockey team! My mom dated Jared for a few days last summer, and every time he came to the house he gave me a regulation Fort Wayne Warriors hockey puck. By the end I had five pucks! Once I ran into him in the kitchenette in the middle of the night. He was making a sandwich. I couldn't believe there was a real hockey player in my house. I wanted to say something, but I was too nervous so I just stood there. Then after a while he looked at me and said, "Hey, little buddy. How's your skating?" And I said, "Fine!"

4. Olaf Seidenberg

Olaf wasn't as strong as Jared, but he was just as cool because he also played hockey for the Fort Wayne Warriors! He only dated my mom once, so I only had one chance to talk to him. Still, it was pretty awesome. It was in the middle of the night. I couldn't sleep, so I went to the kitchenette and *there he was,* Olaf Seidenberg, in *my* house! I asked him to sign my regulation pucks and he said he would. He couldn't believe I had so many pucks! "Wow, kid," he said, "you're a real fan." He autographed all five of them and wrote "16" next to his name, which is his number!

3. Martin Pavlovsky

This guy also played hockey for the Fort Wayne Warriors! He had four goals and two assists in 2006–2007, which isn't great but it was only his first year. When I asked him to sign my regulation Fort Wayne Warriors pucks next to Olaf's signature, he made a weird scrunched-up face and stared at my mother for a while, like he was confused. I guess he doesn't understand a lot of English because he's from the Czech Republic.

2. BILL PASSMAN

This guy played for the Fort Wayne Warriors. He was an okay goalie, but he had some bad luck so his save percentage was only .899. I liked him because his name has the word "Pass" in it, which is a hockey word—and he plays hockey. I only saw Bill once, in the kitchenette. I couldn't believe there was a real hockey player in my house! So I ran into my bedroom and grabbed the old cigar box I use to hold my pucks. When I came back with the box, my mother kept saying that I should go to bed. "Not now, Milo," she started shouting. "Please!" She can be really strict. Anyway, I could tell Bill wanted to see what was in the box so I opened it. "Wow," he said, "you must be my number one fan!" I gave him a puck and told him to sign it next to Olaf's and Nicolas's signatures. (Nicolas was another one of my mom's boyfriends, but he didn't make the top five.) At first he looked a little confused. He said something under his breath, and I was scared he wasn't going to sign my pucks at all. But then he took out a pen and signed *all of them*! It was weird, because he didn't look at the pucks when he signed them. Instead, the whole time he was staring at my mother. His signature was pretty cool—better than Nicolas's but not as good as Olaf's.

1. Bobby Lambert

This guy is great at hockey! He had forty points in the 2006–2007 season with my favorite hockey team, the Fort Wayne Warriors. He went out with my mom for almost two weeks. I didn't get to see him very often because my mom had made a rule that I couldn't leave my room when her boyfriends were over. Still, one night I decided to sneak out of my room and wait in the kitchenette. I mean, how many chances do you get to see a real hockey player in your own house? When I showed Bobby my puck collection, he was super-impressed. "What the hell is going on?" he kept saying. "What the goddamn hell is going on?" Then he looked at my mom and started to cry! It was awesome because I always feel ashamed when I cry. But I thought, If a guy like Bobby Lambert can cry, an AHL all-star center with thirty-five assists, then it's okay if I do too. Bobby kept crying and I was so blown away that I started crying too. And when I went over to him, he hugged me with his huge arms and it was like I had just scored a goal and he had given me the assist.

my friend's new girlfriend

My friend Jared found a girlfriend this summer, and I am *so* jealous. We're the two least popular kids in the ninth grade and we've always been best friends. But now Jared's always bragging about his girlfriend and how awesome she is. It makes me feel so pathetic.

I've never had a girlfriend before, but this girl sounds incredible. Her name is Tiffany Sparkle. She goes to a different school, a modeling academy in New Brunswick. He showed me some pictures of her from magazines, and believe me, she is *hot*. He met her over the summer, when he was visiting his grandparents in Canada. He saved her life. She was about to get run over by a double-decker bus when all of a sudden Jared skateboarded through traffic and pushed her out of the way. There was a huge crowd of Canadians standing around, and when Jared saved

Tiffany's life everybody just started cheering like crazy. Then she kissed him on the mouth. When I heard that story, I was like "Give me a break!" because it was just about the coolest thing I had ever heard in my entire life! They spent the rest of the summer having sex all over the place in all of the different sex positions. And now they talk every night on the phone.

The amazing thing about this girl is that she isn't just hot. She also shares a lot of Jared's interests. She's totally into Web design and the game Warcraft. And she's also really shy. For example, when she visited Jared over spring break, she didn't want to meet me because she was too embarrassed. When I heard that, I was like "Come on!" because that is *so* like Jared. It's kind of amazing that they found each other.

There are other similarities too. Like, he showed me a letter she wrote him last week about how she wanted to try out some new kind of sex position, and at first I thought he had written it *himself* because their handwritings are *so* similar. Tiffany also has severe bronchial asthma, which is pretty great for Jared, because now he has someone to talk to about that.

The big ninth grade dance is in four days. I asked Jared to set me up with one of Tiffany's friends from her modeling academy, but he said that everybody there already has a boyfriend. I asked him for advice on how to find a date, but all of his suggestions involved saving girls' lives. In the end, I decided to just walk up to this girl I like named Laura and ask her point-blank if she wanted to go with me. I was so nervous that my arms and legs were shaking really fast like they do in gym class when the teacher says it's my turn to lead stretches. But I asked her anyway and she said yes.

I talk to Laura on the phone every night now, which is pretty great, because Jared never has time to talk to me anymore. *He's* not even going to the dance! Tiffany's flying to the U.S. for one night only and she hates dancing so they're just going to stay home and try out new sex positions. It's amazing. I mean, don't get me wrong. My date Laura is pretty cool, and other than her leg brace she's very attractive, but she's certainly no Canadian model. It's hard to believe that when I'm on the dance floor this Friday, trying to work up the guts to kiss Laura for the first time, Jared's going to be at home in his bedroom making love to the girl of his dreams. Some guys have all the luck.

invisible

People assume that being invisible is fun, what with the free concerts and the constant unspeakable sex acts. But there are some downsides.

Every day has its trials. When I go to use a urinal at a ball game, I have to make sure there's no one waiting behind me. When I ride the subway I always stand, for fear of fat people.

My friends never notice when I get a new haircut. And when I call them on it, their compliments never sound sincere.

When I was a lifeguard, I never got any credit for any of my heroic rescues. It was always "angel this" and "angel that." Same thing when I was a male prostitute.

When I streaked at the '96 Olympics, it wasn't televised and I was impaled by a javelin. Worse, I never received any cash from the TV miniseries *Legend of the Floating Javelin*. When I took the network to court, the judge declared a mistrial and asked to be lobotomized.

It's really hard to earn a living. I got laid off at the museum because my tour groups kept getting lost. Despite my good looks, acting roles are few and far between. The only film part I ever landed was as a nonspeaking extra in *Cast Away*. I didn't get a screen credit, even though I lost forty pounds for the role.

Sometimes, when I'm alone, I think about how great visible life would be. People nodding hello. Cars slowing down. That's usually when I commit a really terrible sexual act of some kind.

crayola co.

—Thanks for coming, Samuel.

—No problem, boss. I'll have those new color names on your desk by five.

—That's fine. Listen, Sam . . . have you been having problems at home?

—Well, actually, yeah. How did you know? Who told you?

—Well . . . to be honest, I could sort of tell by the quality of your work.

—But I've been writing ten crayon titles a day!

—I know, but some of these colors . . . Sad Blue . . . Sad Green . . . Horrible Red . . . Sad Red . . . Really Sad Blue . . . Divorce Sienna . . . Divorce Brown . . . Divorce Green . . . Divorce Pink . . . It's just . . . a little repetitive, you know?

—Well, all the colors have been more or less the same lately. What can I say? When it comes to crayon naming, you have to go with your first instinct. Like, look at this new shade of orange. What pops into your mind?

—I don't know . . . sunshine?

—Well, yeah. Or divorce. I would say Divorce Orange. Except there already is a Divorce Orange. So then . . . I guess, no name. Just a nameless color.

—I think maybe you need a vacation.

—Really?

—Look, to be honest, last month's colors were a little off too. Adultery Red . . . Ultimatum Pink . . . Lawyers Green . . . Settlement Blue . . . Countersettlement Light Blue . . . Maybe you need to take some time away from the office. You know, to resolve the crisis in your marriage?

—Look, boss. No offense, but I'm just not buying all this psychobabble. I mean, Craig came up with Ladybug Red today. That doesn't mean he has a bug problem at home or whatever.

—Okay. But what about your colors from *two* months ago? Temptation Red? Considering Adultery Blue? Considering Adultery Yellow?

—What about them?

—I think you should take the rest of the day off.

—Okay, you're the boss. I guess I'll see you divorce.

—Do you mean . . . "I'll see you tomorrow?"

—That's what I said.

"may or may not contain peanuts"

—Boss? I got to talk to you. It's about Al. I think it's time for him to retire.

—Peanut Al? No way. That guy's been the heart and soul of this factory for decades.

—I know, but he's really dropping the ball out there. His only job is to put peanuts into the batter. And half the time *he forgets*.

—I know! It's just . . . Al used to be the best peanut man in the business. I can't throw him out onto the streets! Even if he is ninety-seven.

—Hello, boss. Peanut Al here.

—Hi, Al! How are you holding up?

—I don't remember if I added the peanuts or not.

—Jesus.

—Peanut Al is going home to sleep. Tired as all hell.

—All right. Goodbye, Al.

—Peanut Al needs to get some rest. You know what? I don't remember a goddamn thing that happened today. I might've put *something* in the batter. Not peanuts.

—Wow.

—See you tomorrow.

—See what I mean, boss? What are we going to do?

—I don't know. I guess we'll have to figure out something to write on the label.

medieval england

In medieval England, all measurements were based on the king's body parts.

AT THE CRICKET MATCH

—Wow, he tossed that over thirty feet!

—Thirty *Henry* feet?

—No. Thirty *James* feet.

—Oh. That's only ten Henry feet.

—I know. Or five Henry thumbs.

—Henry was a terrifying man.

—Let's not talk about him.

AT THE TAILOR

—I'd like a suit.

—No problem. How tall are you?

—Let's see . . . about one king tall.

—Can you be more specific?

—Well, actually, no.

—Dammit.

—I also need some gloves. My hands are . . . about one hand long.

—Yes, I can see that.

AT THE DOCTOR

—Your blood pressure is two Henrys.

—Is that good or bad?

—It's really bad.

patron of the arts

Donate to the City Museum now and you'll receive the following benefits!

FRIEND (CONTRIBUTIONS OF $1–$49)
- Official City Museum Badge.
- A private tour of the City Museum, conducted by the Head Curator.

PATRON (CONTRIBUTIONS OF $50–$299)
- Official City Museum Tie.
- Invitation to have tea with the Head Curator and his family at his private residence.

ANGEL (CONTRIBUTIONS OF $300–$799)
- Permission to destroy any work of art and replace it with your own work.

• The Head Curator will perform a dance for you in front of his peers.

MESSIAH (CONTRIBUTIONS OF $800–$2,999)
• The Head Curator will come to your house and make you dinner. After dinner he will massage your back with oils.
• The Head Curator will dance for you twice, once in front of his peers and once in front of his own children.

PHARAOH (CONTRIBUTIONS OF $3,000–$24,999)
• Whenever the Head Curator sees you, he will salute, curtsy, and then run in place until you motion for him to stop.
• Unlimited dances.

WARLORD
(CONTRIBUTIONS OF $25,000 AND UP)
• One night with the Head Curator's wife.
• Whenever you snap your fingers, the Head Curator will drop whatever it is he is doing and burst spontaneously into song.
• 15% discount at Gift Shop.

baseball's hardest worker

Nobody in the history of baseball had it rougher than Cy Young, the most durable pitcher the game has ever known.

CLEVELAND STADIUM DUGOUT, 1904
CY: I don't know if I can handle another triple-header. Couldn't we have some sort of rotation system?
MANAGER: What's with you today, Cy? You haven't sold a single hot dog, the dugout's filthy, the scoreboard's busted. That's three strikes. You only have five strikes left.
CY: Can we please lower the number of strikes per out?
MANAGER: Strike four, Cy.

LATER THAT DAY

CY: Tomorrow's my seventy-fifth birthday. Can I please have the day off?

MANAGER: Can't do that, Cy. We've got fifty games tomorrow and you're pitching all of them.

CY: Oh my God. Who's catching?

MANAGER: Who's *what*?

CHILDREN'S HOSPITAL WARD

CY: So, how many strikeouts is it going to take for you to walk again?

SICK BOY: I need two kidneys.

CY: What?

DOCTOR: Remove the jersey.

orel hershiser

I'd like to thank God for this victory.
I couldn't have done it without him.
—OREL HERSHISER, L.A. Dodgers

ANGEL: God? Can I talk to you for a second?

GOD: I'm watching the game.

ANGEL: I know—I'm sorry for interrupting. I just wanted to tell you: There's been a flood in Asia. Four hundred thousand people have lost their homes.

GOD: Listen, I don't think you understand. Orel Hershiser is on the mound. If he wins this game, he'll improve his record to 13–3. That's ten games over .500.

ANGEL: I know, I'm sorry, it's just . . . If we don't act in the next thirty minutes, thousands of people might drown.

GOD: Slide, Martinez! Slide, dammit! I'm sorry . . . I wasn't listening. What were you saying?

ANGEL: If you don't stop the rains soon, thousands will die. They've been praying all night. I really think you should answer them.

GOD: It looks like I'm going to have to intervene.

ANGEL: Really? Oh, that's great news!

ANNOUNCER: *Orel Hershiser winds up . . . Strike three! Wow—that fastball came out of nowhere!*

GOD: Boo-yah! That's what I'm talking about!

ANGEL: When you said you were going to intervene . . . were you talking about the baseball game or the flood?

GOD: What flood?

ANGEL: (sighing) There's been a flood in Asia. Hundreds of thousands of people—

GOD: Shit! Hold on a second . . . I need to concentrate.

ANNOUNCER: *Mike Piazza pounds Hershiser's curveball into deep right field! He's rounding second . . . he should get to third base easily . . . Oh no! He's down! His leg just buckled underneath him! He's screaming now . . . wow . . . he really seems to be in a lot of pain. Here comes the tag . . . he's out. Looks like the Dodgers are the winners. Although I'm sure they didn't want to win like this.*

ANGEL: Okay, the game's over. Can we please talk about the flood now?

GOD: In a second. I want to hear the postgame interview.

HERSHISER: *I'd like to thank God for this victory. I couldn't have done it without him.*

GOD: Hey, did you hear that! Did you hear what he just said!

ANGEL: Yes, I heard.

GOD: Man . . . I *love* that Hershiser guy.

ANGEL: Can we talk about the flood now?

GOD: In a minute. NASCAR's on. I got to make sure Greg Biffle wins.

ANGEL: Do you really have to watch NASCAR?

GOD: Yes! I don't think you get it. There are people out there who are counting on me.

if life were like hockey

POLICE OFFICER: I can't believe it! You just hit that man, deliberately, with a stick. Right in the back, as hard as you could! You didn't even try to hide what you were doing.

CRAZY PERSON: What are you going to do about it?

POLICE OFFICER: I'm . . . going to make you sit on that bench. For two minutes.

CRAZY PERSON: Can I bring along my stick?

POLICE OFFICER: Yes.

CRAZY PERSON: Sounds good. (To victim) I'll see you in two minutes.

VICTIM: Officer! What am I supposed to do?

POLICE OFFICER: I don't know. Fight him?

colombiatourism.com

Thank you for visiting ColombiaTourism.com! Here are some useful phrases for your vacation. Click on them for English-to-Spanish translations.

"Which way to the restaurant?"

"How much does it cost?"

"Where is the bathroom?

"Who are you?"

"Oh my God, where are you taking me?"

"Please do not put the rag inside of my mouth."

"My father is a wealthy man. I promise he will pay the amount you have requested, provided that you spare my life."

"I have not seen your face. If you release me, I promise, I will not be able to identify you."

"I have a family whom I love. Deep down, I am like you."

"I agree with your sentiments about America. Your philosophy is correct and very reasonable."

"I feel a strong emotional bond toward you, even though you are my captor."

"With every passing day, we are becoming better friends. Say, that is a unique gun. May I see it?"

"Thank you."

"The tables have turned!"

"Do not move while I put the chains on you. I will shoot!"

"Officer! Three men tried to kidnap me. Arrest them at once."

"What are you doing? Why are you putting the handcuffs on me?"

"Oh my God, you are in league with the kidnappers. How can this be? Is there no law in this land?"

"Yes, I will stop talking."

ant farm

—All right men, listen up. As you know, we've built seven tunnels and we still haven't found a way through the glass. I can tell you're discouraged and I don't blame you. Tunnel 7 was our most ambitious project to date and you all risked your lives to make it happen. But rest assured, we'll be out of this hellish wasteland soon enough. I have a plan.

—What is it? What's the plan?

—An eighth tunnel. Through the sand.

—I don't know, sir . . . we've been digging tunnels ever since we got here. We always end up hitting glass. We lost ten men on the last tunnel: Brian, Jack, Lawrence—

—I know their names.

—Why don't we just give up? I mean seriously, what's the point?

—The point? The point is we have no food or water. The point is we're trapped in this crazy desert, and if we don't find an exit soon we're going to suffocate.

—What kind of God would put us here, just to torture us? Sand to the left . . . sand to the right . . .

—It's a test, William. He's testing us.

—You're right. We can do this. We just have to work ten times harder than we've ever worked before! (Starts digging.)

—You want to know something? I've got a good feeling about this one. A really good feeling.

IV

love coupons

—Brian? What are you doing here?

—I came to redeem some coupons.

—(reading) "Good for one back rub" . . . "Good for one home-cooked meal" . . . Brian, I gave these to you while we were still dating.

—There's no expiration date on the coupons.

—Brian, it's been four years. I'm married now.

—One home-cooked meal, please. Then sex. Here . . . here's the sex one. One of the sex ones.

—Brian, I'm sorry. It's over between us.

—Coupons are coupons.

—Wow, Brian . . . you've really gained a lot of weight. Is everything okay?

—I've got three sex coupons. I'd like to use them all

today, then the meal, then the shower. Tomorrow, I'll come back with the rest of the coupons. They're all sex.

—Jesus, what happened to your *nails*? I can't believe I didn't notice them when I first opened the door. They're *so long*.

—I would like to use a sex one now please.

stadium proposal

Last night at Cowboys Stadium, Graham Baxter pro-
posed to his girlfriend, Jennifer, in front of forty-one
thousand screaming fans.

"Look up," he said. "There's something I want you to
see."

There it was, in ten-foot neon lights:

JENNIFER, WILL YOU MARRY ME?

"Of course!" she squealed. "Of course I will, darling!"

There were two other Jennifers at the game.

SECTION 26, ROW 19

JENNIFER: Of course I will, Michael! Of course!

MICHAEL: Huh? Where are you pointing? . . . Oh, no!
Oh, God!

JENNIFER: I have three children who you've never met
and two of them have bad problems.

SECTION 45, ROW 11

JENNIFER: Danny, we've had some rough patches . . .
but . . . yes! My answer is yes!

DANNY: What do you mean? Oh—oh, no! (crying) *Who
did this!?*

JENNIFER: God. My magical Druid God.

DANNY: . . .

JENNIFER: The ceremony has to be Druid.

sultan of brunei

The Sultan of Brunei is the richest oil magnate in the world. Servants, yachts, castles—he's got everything! Everything except true love.

GIRLFRIEND: What's wrong, honey?

SULTAN: Well . . . it's just . . . sometimes I think you're only going out with me because of my money.

GIRLFRIEND: Oh, darling! How could you say something like that?

SULTAN: What do you mean? I can say whatever I want. I'm the Sultan of Brunei.

GIRLFRIEND: You're right, I'm sorry.

SULTAN: Get back into your fortress of rubies.

SULTAN: Honey, if I ask you a question, will you promise to tell me the truth?

CONCUBINE: Of course!

SULTAN: Would you still love me if I were poor? Keep in mind that if you say no, one of my warriors will murder you.

CONCUBINE: Yes, I would love you no matter what!

SULTAN: Okay, good. Now . . . do you want to see a movie or go bowling? Keep in mind that if you say bowling, one of my warriors will murder you.

CONCUBINE: Let's see a movie.

SULTAN: I am the Sultan of Brunei!

SULTAN: I'm sorry I missed our anniversary, honey. Things were crazy at the office. I was counting gold bars and—

WIFE: You didn't even get me a present!

SULTAN: Yes I did! I got you . . . this . . . drum of crude oil.

WIFE: That's not going to work this time.

SULTAN: You're so unforgiving! What happened to the woman I married?

WIFE: Which one? You have two hundred wives.

SULTAN: The one with the ribbons.

WIFE: She's downstairs, I think.

SULTAN: Oh. What about Sheila?

WIFE: I'm Sheila.

SULTAN: Oh.

(Pause.)

SULTAN: Bear me a child of solid gold.

endangered species

Last year, the San Francisco Zoo attempted to mate
their endangered striped panda with three females from
other zoos in an effort to perpetuate the species.
But their venture failed, and ultimately
the striped panda became extinct.
—SAN FRANCISCO CHRONICLE

ATTEMPT 1

Hi, nice to meet you! Welcome to San Francisco! God, these blind dates are pretty awkward! It's really nice of the zookeepers to set us up like this, though, huh? I guess they're probably hoping that we'll mate! (Pause.) I'm sorry. That was really out of bounds. Wow, I can't believe I said something so thoughtless. You must think I'm a total idiot. Jesus, and now I'm making it even worse. And that—*that last thing I said*—made it *even worse!* God, this is so humiliating.

ATTEMPT 2

. . . I'm the kind of guy who doesn't take himself too seriously. A lot of other animals around here like to strut around and growl, but I don't buy into any of that. That's not to say I can't growl loudly. I can.

So this is my rock. I like to do my exercises here. I don't work out *too* much, I'm not obsessive or anything. I climb the rock about fifty or sixty times a day. I mean, sure, for *some* guys that would be a lot. But for me it isn't. Climbing the rock is pretty easy for me.

See those bleachers? During the daytime, they're full of kids. The zookeeper gives me a treat every time I do my trick, but you want to know something? I would do the trick for free, just to see the smiles on those kids' faces. That's just the kind of guy I am.

Do you want to see my trick? No? Okay, that's cool. Are you sure? Okay.

Say, that's a nice ankle tag you got on! It really looks good . . . on your ankle. God, I always do this. I do this every time.

ATTEMPT 3

. . . Maybe I'm old-fashioned, but I think female striped pandas deserve the same amount of respect as male striped pandas. I mean sure, males can growl louder and climb the rock more times, but it's what's deep down that counts. I guess you could say that's kind of my philosophy on life.

Look at me, talking your head off! You must be hungry. Hold on, I'll get the zookeeper's attention. (Growls.) Okay . . . I guess he didn't hear me. We might have to wait a while.

So, your tag says you're from Siberia? That's pretty cool! Do you have a lot of brothers and sisters there? Oh, right . . . of course you don't. I'm sorry.

mating throughout history

Stone Age

SCRAWNY GUY: Hi! I was wondering . . . do you want to mate with me?

WOMAN: I don't think so. You're not really my type. I'm looking for a guy with really big muscles. You know, the kind of guy who can build me a fort and protect my children from forest beasts. I'm sorry.

SCRAWNY GUY: It's cool . . . That's actually pretty reasonable. See you around.

WOMAN: See ya.

Present Day

SCRAWNY GUY: Hi! I was wondering . . . can I buy you a drink after work?

WOMAN: I don't think so. You're not really my type. I'm

looking for a guy with really big muscles. You know, the kind of guy who can build me a fort and protect my children from forest beasts. I'm sorry.

SCRAWNY GUY: What? That doesn't make any sense. We live in a *city*, thousands of miles away from the nearest forest.

WOMAN: I'm sorry. I'm just not attracted to you.

THE FUTURE

SCRAWNY GUY: Hi! I was wondering . . . do you want to drink some purified water with me after this asteroid barrage stops?

WOMAN: I don't think so. You're not really my type. I'm looking for a guy with really big muscles. You know, the kind of guy who can build me a fort and protect my children from forest beasts.

SCRAWNY GUY: What forest beasts? We're the last remaining species on the planet!

WOMAN: I'm sorry. I'm just not attracted to you.

SCRAWNY GUY: Listen, I have a unique genetic mutation that allows me to breathe radon gas like it was air! I'm the only person on earth who can survive the nuclear winter. If you don't mate with me, all human life will die out!

THE LAST MUSCULAR GUY ON EARTH: (coughing from the radon gas) Hey, baby. Nice ass.

WOMAN: (Giggles.)

SCRAWNY GUY: What's happening? This is completely insane.

THE LAST MUSCULAR GUY ON EARTH: (sweating) Let's go to my fort, babe. (Cough.) I built it out of rocks, using my muscle arms.

WOMAN: Whatever you say, lover.

when the
"guess your weight" guy
from the carnival got married

—Darling, can I ask you a question?

—Sure.

—Do you think I gained any weight over the holidays?

—I don't know. I can't tell.

—We've been over this. I know you can tell.

—You look as beautiful as ever!

—I was 119 pounds in October. How much do you think I weigh now?

—Why are you doing this to me?

—Tell me the truth.

—Okay! All right! You gained 11 pounds, give or take 3 pounds! Is that what you wanted to hear? Jesus Christ!

—I knew it. You think I'm fat. That's why you've been flirting with that Debbie girl from work. Even though she's *half your age.*

—I wasn't flirting with her! And she's *not* half my age. You can tell just by looking at her that she's 27, give or take 3 years.

—(Sobbing.)

—Hey, come on! Why are we fighting? *I love you.* When I'm out there on the midway every night, guessing people's weights and ages, I'm doing it for you! I'm doing it for our kids!

—I'm sorry. I didn't mean to start a fight. (Kisses him.) Little Tommy sure is growing up, isn't he?

—4 foot 4, give or take 3 inches.

—And Suzy! I can't believe how adult she's getting.

—14 to 17 years old.

—Wait. You don't know how old our daughter is?

—Jesus Christ, I'm not a computer! (Sighs.) Look . . . I'm sorry, okay? Here. I got you a giant stuffed animal.

—That's not going to work this time.

my roommate is really hard to get along with

ROOMMATE: What happened to my chips?

ME: Oh, I ate some while you were in the bathroom. I'm sorry, I should have asked first.

ROOMMATE: You have the right to remain silent. Anything you say may be used against you in a court of law.

ME: Not this again . . .

ROOMMATE: I'm making a citizen's arrest.

ME: *Come on!*

ROOMMATE: (dialing) Police? Yeah, it's me. I got a live one for you, 119 Elmer Street.

ME: You can't keep doing this! This is the fourth time this week!

ROOMMATE: (hanging up) The cops are on their way. In the meantime, I'm going to have to ask you to wait in the citizen's jail.

ME: You mean the kitchenette?

ROOMMATE: Yes.

(Policeman enters.)

POLICEMAN: I understand there's been a crime?

ROOMMATE: That's right. I placed this man under arrest. He's a thief.

POLICEMAN: Do you want me to take him to the courthouse, or just rough him up a little?

ROOMMATE: Rough him up.

homework

—Hey man, can you help me out with my math home-
work?

—Sure.

—Great, thanks. On problem 7, am I supposed to take
the sine or the cosine of this angle?

—Let me think . . . Stab and Obliterate the Hebrews,
Crucify All the Hebrews, Triumph Over All . . . I guess
it's the cosine.

—Wait—what did you just say?

—Cosine.

—No, before that. About the Hebrews?

—Oh, that's just a mnemonic device I came up with.
"Stab" stands for "sine," "Obliterate" stands for "oppo-
site leg of," "Hebrews" stands for "hypotenuse."

—Oh. Well, couldn't you have picked a device that's . . .

less hateful? I mean, as a Jew I'm pretty offended by what you just said.

—Really? Those words are totally random. I just picked them because they started with the right letters.

—Yeah, I guess you're right. I'm sorry, I overreacted.

—It's okay. Let's try another problem.

—Cool. So, in problem 9, do you know which operation we're supposed to do first? Is it exponents or division?

—Let me think . . . Permanently Eliminate Many Jews, Destroy All Synagogues . . . You do exponents first.

—What the hell was that?

—Oh, that was just another mnemonic: Parentheses, Exponents, Multiplication, Division, Addition, Subtraction.

—But that one doesn't even work! The word "Jew" doesn't stand in for anything!

—Yeah, you're right. I guess it's sort of like a placeholder?

—Well, it's *really* offensive.

—I don't know what to tell you. Maybe "Jew" could stand in for "'jacent?" You know, like, short for "adjacent"?

—But then it doesn't make sense mathematically.

—I'm not changing the mnemonic.

when small talk goes wrong

—Did you see who won the game?
—I was at the game. A ball hit my son in the face. He's in critical condition at Mt. Sinai Hospital. The doctors say he might not make it. So, in answer to your question: No. I have no idea who won the game.

—Hey, you look familiar. Have we met?
—Oh my God, I've gained so much weight that you didn't even recognize me. This is the single most humiliating experience of my life. *We dated for seven years.*

—Do you have the time?
—Shh! It's 4:26 P.M.!
—Huh?
—(whispering) April twenty-sixth, 4:26 P.M., is an official

minute of silence. Congress created it to honor the 426 men who died in the Great Boise Fire. My father was among those men.

—Oh my God, I'm so sorry. I'll stop talking.

—It doesn't matter. The minute has already passed.

—What are you drinking?

—It's a cocktail of seven medications. If I don't drink one of these every thirty seconds, my eyeballs rupture. Oh no . . . *How long have we been talking?*

—Do you come here often?

—Yes. My brother was murdered at this bar in 1983. I come every year on the anniversary of his death to say a prayer. I miss him so much. I know he's gone, but part of me still can't let go. He was stabbed to death in the neck.

—Are you on the bride's side or the groom's?

—Well, the groom is my brother, and the bride is my wife . . . I'm sorry, I mean *ex*-wife. God, that's going to take some getting used to. I still love her, you know. Even after what she did. (Drinks an entire glass of champagne.) You want to know something? This is the worst day of my life.

jesus

JESUS: Love each other, for love conquers all.

THOMAS: Praise the Lord!

JESUS: If someone attacks you, turn the other cheek.

THOMAS: Praise the Lord!

JESUS: Eat my body and my blood.

THOMAS: Praise the— Wait. What was that last thing?

JESUS: Eat my body and my blood.

THOMAS: You mean . . . symbolically?

JESUS: No.

THOMAS: Oh.

JESUS: Honor thy father and thy mother.

THOMAS: Wait, hold on. Can we talk about that other thing for a second?

JESUS: What other thing? Turning the other cheek?

THOMAS: No, the thing you said after. About eating your body . . . and . . . your blood.

JESUS: What's there to talk about?

karma

When I told my friends I was converting to Hinduism, they said I was rushing into things. They're just jealous because I'm racking up karma points left and right. Check out today's tally:

9:00 A.M. Brushed teeth.	+2
9:25 A.M. Helped an old woman cross the street.	+50
9:30 A.M. Rubbed old woman's belly in order to absorb some of her karma.	+20
10:00 A.M. Bet my buddy Greg 50 karmas that I could beat him in a vodka-chugging race.	+50

10:04 A.M. Made awesome "Karma and Greg" joke.	+200
1:00 P.M. Went to homeless shelter.	+100
1:01 P.M. Pretended to be homeless in order to receive free soup.	−10
1:05 P.M. Traded the soup to a real homeless man in exchange for all his karmas.	+3,500
5:00 P.M. Constructed Hindu idol out of styrofoam.	+75
5:45 P.M. Carried the styrofoam idol to a Hindu temple and threatened to destroy it if the priests didn't give me all of their karmas.	+35,000
8 P.M. Stole.	−15
11:00 P.M. Vegetarian snack.	+20
Next Life	= Dragon

repent

According to evangelical Christians, anyone who accepts Jesus Christ as his personal Lord and Savior will enter the Kingdom of Heaven. Even murderers can enter Heaven, as long as they have faith. As you can imagine, it gets pretty awkward up there when murderers run into people that they've killed.

MURDERER: Hey, you look familiar. Do I know you from somewhere?

VICTIM: (Terrified screaming.)

MURDERER: Oh, yeah. Now I remember.

VICTIM: How did you get up here?

MURDERER: I'm not really sure. Someone sent me a Bible while I was on death row. I guess at some point I must have internalized parts of it?

VICTIM: So . . . they gave you the death penalty?

MURDERER: Yeah. Not for killing you, though. For killing some other people. Children.

VICTIM: Oh.

MURDERER: Nobody knows you're dead yet. I hid you in a weird place.

VICTIM: . . .

MURDERER: Listen, I'm really sorry about what happened. If it makes you feel any better, I told a priest about it afterward. He made me say, like, fifty prayers.

VICTIM: How many people did you murder?

MURDERER: Four hundred. But I've only run into three or four of them so far. I guess not everyone makes it into Heaven, huh? Hey look, there's Jesus.

JESUS: Well, well, well, if it isn't the Prodigal Son! (Laughs, puts arm around murderer's shoulder.) Seriously, it's great to have you aboard.

MURDERER: Jesus, I want you to meet someone. This is . . . um . . . geez. This is pretty embarrassing. What's your name again?

JESUS: Sorry I can't stay and meet your friend, but I have to go welcome in some other murderers. So long!

MURDERER: Guess he was in a rush, huh? Oh well. I'll try to introduce you some other time.

a conversation between god and the man in a football helmet and a speedo who's always shouting things next to the a&p

—How'd it go today? Win any followers?

—I'm afraid not, God. I'm sorry.

—You told them the news, right? That the world is ending in four days?

—Yes.

—And you made the sign, like I told you? With all the information about the apocalypse?

—Of course.

—Did you try that thing I came up with, where you start swinging your arms around really fast while saying "The end is coming, the end is coming"?

—(sighing) Yes.

—And still no one listened! I can't believe this. How can I prepare mankind for the apocalypse if they ignore the words of my prophet?

—I actually had a thought today, God. I was thinking, maybe if I wore something a little more socially acceptable . . .

—I have a strict dress code for my prophets: helmet, Speedo.

—I know, I don't mean to second-guess you! I just think people would respond better if I wore a suit.

—Did you do the thing where you start hitting your helmet with both fists to get people's attention, and then when they finally look at you, you just start screaming and pointing at the sign?

—Yes. A lot.

—Then I guess we have no choice. Construct a gown out of aluminum foil and gird yourself with it.

—Again?

—Do as I say.

—I really don't think that's going to work.

—Of course it will! Think about it. If you saw a guy dressed entirely in foil, would you ignore him? No. You'd sit down and listen to what he had to say.

—Listen, God, I'm honored that you chose me to be your prophet—and it's been a really exciting thirty-five years, don't get me wrong. But I'm starting to think that maybe you should ask someone else to deliver your message. Like a senator, maybe? Or a minister?

—Impossible. You are the prophet I have chosen.

—Well, maybe I should at least leave the A&P. The manager keeps sending out someone with a broom to chase me off the lot. It's pretty humiliating.

—Yeah, I saw that. That was pretty bad.

—Did you see when all the foil fell off while I was running away? So that I was completely naked, except for the helmet?

—Yeah. That probably set us back a little. Maybe you should move to the side of the highway? I'm sure we'll have more luck there.

—Okay.

—And I want you to make your sign bigger.

—Sure.

—And one more thing.

—What?

—Keep your head up.

—(Laughs.) Thanks, God.

the odds

The odds of winning the lottery are statistically equal to the odds of getting mauled by a circus animal. The last guy to win the lottery was Al Romano. He won $80 million playing Powerball. The last guy to get mauled by a circus animal was Sam Ortle. He was attacked by a bear. I thought it would be neat to introduce these guys.

ME: Well, I'm sure you guys have a lot to talk about. See you later! (Exits.)

AL: Hi.

SAM: Hi. Congratulations on winning the lottery.

AL: Thanks! I'm really sorry . . . about your misfortune.

SAM: It had to happen to someone, I guess.

AL: How did it happen, exactly? Do you work for the circus?

SAM: No, I work for a computer company on the other side of town. I just happened to be out on my lunch break when the bear escaped into the city. I bent over to tie my shoes, and when I stood up he was sprinting toward me with both arms in the air. It was the single most terrifying moment of my life.

AL: I'm so sorry.

SAM: Yeah. I guess I was just in the wrong place at the wrong time. So . . . how much money did you win in the lottery?

AL: Eighty million dollars. It sounds like more than it is, though! I have to pay a lot of taxes! (Long silence.) Listen, again, I'm really sorry about the bear. The whole thing sounds terrible. How did it escape in the first place?

SAM: An earthquake broke open his cage. Then two lightning bolts knocked the guards unconscious. It's sort of like God was doing everything he could that day to make sure this horrible thing would happen to me.

AL: Jesus.

SAM: So . . . do you buy lottery tickets often?

AL: Actually, this was my first time. I was in a store and I saw the "World's Biggest Jackpot" sign so I just kind of bought one on a whim.

SAM: I buy lottery tickets pretty often. About five or six a week. I still haven't won anything.

AL: Why do you keep looking over your shoulder like that?

SAM: Checking for bears. I know it probably won't happen again, but I don't want to take any chances. It's a crazy world. Hey, what are you going to do with all the money?

AL: I haven't really decided. I'm still a little dazed by the whole thing!

SAM: You know what I would do if I won the lottery? I'd build myself a suit to protect against bears. I'd wear it all the time, for the rest of my life.

AL: You know, if you want, I could buy you a suit with my winnings! Seriously, I'd be happy to do it.

SAM: What's the point? Some bear would find a way.

where are all the time travelers?

Stephen Hawking once said, "If time travel is real, where are all the time travelers?" Everyone I talk to thinks this is such a great quote and that it proves that time travel is just a fantasy. But what people are forgetting is that Stephen Hawking is obviously a time traveler.

Think about it. "If time travel is real, where are all the time travelers?" *That is exactly the kind of thing a time traveler would say.* Everyone's like "Oh, Stephen Hawking, you're so smart, of course there's no such thing as time travel!" Meanwhile, Hawking is probably at the dog track right now winning trifecta after trifecta.

Let's think about this rationally. If you were a time traveler who had visited the future, and someone asked you point-blank if time travel was possible, what would you say? "Oh, yeah, time travel is definitely possible. In fact, *I'm* a time traveler—confiscate my gambling earnings"? No. You would make some witty quip and change the subject. Then you would politely excuse yourself, call a bookie, and bet on Duke to defeat UNLV in the 1991 NCAA semifinals, even though they were eleven-point underdogs.

Where are all the time travelers? They're on Wall Street, smoking Cuban cigars and laughing so hard that tears are streaming down their fat faces. Meanwhile, *we're* sitting around like morons, betting our money on random dogs and horses and talking about how smart Stephen Hawking is. He probably didn't even write his books! If you could magically travel through time, think about how easy it would be to bring back some smart book from the future, retype it, and pass it off as your own.

The following people are also probably time travelers:

- the woman who married Bill Gates before he invented Microsoft
- the guy who just *happened* to be filming JFK when he got assassinated
- George Foreman (how else would he know to sponsor that grill?)

There have always been time travelers. And anyone who says otherwise probably has something to hide.

desert island

I was chatting with a girl at a cocktail party last weekend and she asked me, "If you were stranded on a desert island and you could only take three possessions with you, which ones would you pick?"

"That's pretty tough," I said. "I guess my first-edition copy of Bob Dylan's *Highway 61 Revisited,* James Merrill's *Collected Poems,* and my lucky Sonic Youth T-shirt."

Well, it turns out the girl was a government research scientist. It's a long story, but basically when the drugs in my cocktail wore off, I woke up completely naked on a sandy strip of land in the middle of the ocean. A few hours later a jet plane whizzed by and parachute-dropped the record, book, and shirt onto the shore.

I realize now that I definitely could have chosen better items.

The last three days have been hell. I have no food, shelter, or medicine. The Sonic Youth T-shirt has an enormous tear through the front. It's pretty cool-looking, and it shows I've had the shirt for a long time, since before Sonic Youth got big. But the tear lets in *a lot* of cold air, and the larger insects keep getting trapped in it.

Every few hours I flip through the Merrill anthology in the hope that one of his poems will be about fire building or water purification or how to make medicine, but so far they're all useless.

I spent yesterday morning tying the Bob Dylan record to a stick with weeds and swinging it over my head to try to receive radio waves. I don't remember why I thought that would work.

If I had asked for a Bob Dylan *CD*, I could have at least used the reflective surface to maybe heat up some sand. I'm not sure what that would accomplish, but at least I'd feel like I was *doing* something.

This morning I ate the poetry book and the shirt. Tonight, I'm going to try to eat the record.

Let me tell you some more about this island. During the daytime, the sand is so hot that I need to constantly hop from foot to foot to prevent my feet from getting burned. At night it's below freezing. There are no trees. There's just sand, weeds, and some kind of volcano. Every fish I've caught so far has been poisonous.

I just realized that, technically, my house counts as a possession. I could have asked for my entire house.

I don't even like Bob Dylan. I just wanted to sound cool.

the dog x-files

Here are some scenes for a TV show I came up with that's exactly like *The X-Files* except all of the characters are dogs.

REX: Thank God you're here. I didn't know who else to turn to. No one believes my story.

DOG SCULLY: Tell us what happened.

REX: I used to go into the living room every day. I'd run around, scratch up the couches—you know, have a good time. Then yesterday, I went inside and all of a sudden a horrible electric shock shot through my entire body.

DOG MULDER: Unbelievable.

DOG SCULLY: Did you try going in again today?

REX: Yes. The same thing happened. I don't even want to go into that room anymore.

DOG MULDER: Wow. I have no explanation.

DOG MULDER: I'm Agent Mulder from the Dog FBI. Tell us what happened.

SKIP: Last week, my face was really itchy. I kept trying to scratch my nose, but . . . I couldn't reach it.

DOG MULDER: What do you mean?

SKIP: There was some kind of cone-shaped force field surrounding my head.

DOG SCULLY: Incredible!

SKIP: The crazy thing is, three days later, I fell asleep . . . and when I woke up, the force field was gone.

DOG SCULLY: I don't understand. This defies all logic!

DOG MULDER: Not everything can be explained with logic, Dog Scully.

BOOMER: This is really hard for me. You're the first people I've told.

DOG SCULLY: Tell us what happened. Maybe we can help.

BOOMER: Okay, here goes. Yesterday I fell asleep, and when I woke up, my testicles were missing.

DOG SCULLY: Jesus. This is the fifth case this month.

DOG MULDER: There's something happening out there. Something beyond our understanding.

ROCKET: I used to have fleas all over my body. Thousands and thousands of them. Then, yesterday, I felt a tightness around my neck . . . and within hours the fleas were gone.

DOG MULDER: (Spits out coffee.)

DOG SCULLY: For years, I've tried to be a scientist, to live by the rules of logic and reason. But now I don't know what to believe.

DOG MULDER: Please use your magic to kill my fleas.

animal cruelty

In order to learn more about animal cruelty, I built a translating machine and interviewed several farm animals about their current situation.

Cow

—You've been incarcerated in this slaughterhouse your entire life. How has it affected you emotionally?

—I am cow. I eat grass. Grass on ground. Me move mouth down to grass. Chew up grass.

—Do you think animal slavery will end in your lifetime?

—Eat grass, rest. Eat grass, rest. Sleep.

—Do you feel that animals deserve the same rights as human beings?

—Grass on ground. Eat it all up.

Chicken

—You've lived inside this 26- × 22-inch cage your entire life. How does it feel to know that you will never meet your family?

—Food in bag. Eat it up.

—Are "free range" chickens truly free? Or do they suffer the same indignities as standard, factory-produced chickens?

—Me eat food in bag. Rest. Sleep.

Pig

—Human beings have mistreated your species for centuries, caging you in tiny prisons and pumping you full of dangerous hormones, just to make money. If you could say one thing to your human oppressors, what would it be?

—Give me more of the things that go inside my mouth. I like the things that I put inside my mouth. Chew it all up good. Rest, sleep.

—I understand that your owner castrated you at birth and then branded you with a fiery hot iron. Does it ever get so bad that you wish for death?

—Give me more of the things that go inside my mouth.

lost puppy!

Our beloved family pet is missing! We lost him on *this block* and he probably hasn't gone far. If you find a dog that matches the following description, please give me a call! Thanks! —Suzie

Large claws

Extra set of teeth

Red eyes

Quick to anger

Often unreasonable; lacks the self-control of other dogs

Likes to stand on his hind legs and rise to his full height
so he can look people in the eye

Often stays in shadowy areas; very hard to spot sometimes, except for his eyes, which always have a faint
red glow

Fast

When he stands on his hind legs and looks people in the
eye, he expects them to maintain eye contact; if they
look away even for a second, he has a kind
of breakdown

If he's having a rampage and someone escapes, he likes
to come find them, usually on the one-year anniversary
of the rampage

Answers to the name "Ctharga," but if his name is said
three times, something weird happens to his eyes and he
somehow becomes even faster than he is normally

Silent

glorious battles of the american revolution

The British redcoats were excellently trained. But their conventional battle tactics failed to subdue the ragtag American troops.

The Battle of Stoney Point — 1779

George Washington's minutemen attack the redcoats with pitchforks. Cornwallis, the British general, stubbornly sticks to his strategy: offering the Americans tea and then cleverly giving them none.

The Battle of Hobkirk's Hill — 1780

The Americans kill five thousand redcoats by hitting them on the head with rocks. Cornwallis and his surviving men retaliate by throwing an elaborate dinner party and not inviting any minutemen. Washington comes anyway. During sherry he makes an extremely lewd toast. Out of politeness, the redcoats pretend not to hear him. But a few minutes later Washington repeats his toast, loudly. One by one, all the redcoats make very courteous excuses and leave early.

THE BATTLE OF GRIME'S RIVER—1781

At 9:30 A.M., the redcoats assemble on the battlefield, but as usual the Americans are tardy. Furious, Cornwallis marches his infantry up to Washington's tent and requests permission to fire his gun at him. Washington, still drunk from the night before, stumbles out of the tent and starts dancing. Cornwallis is enraged, but etiquette demands that he join the dance. The redcoats retreat slowly, careful to avoid any eye contact with Cornwallis.

THE BATTLE OF HAW FOREST—1782

General Washington sets a forest on fire to show Cornwallis that he's ready to fight. As a gesture of good faith, Cornwallis executes his five best men. Washington goes on to win the battle by poisoning some local Indians and forcing them to kill the redcoats in exchange for medicine. In accordance with British military law, Mrs. Cornwallis bakes General Washington a congratulatory scone and invites him to her drawing room for whist. Washington insists on having sex with her. They have sex.

a day in the life
of the swiss army

All right, everyone, listen up. I'm not going to lie to you. We lost a lot of good men today. But we haven't lost the war yet. It's time to hunker down and talk strategy: Has everybody been taking care of his fingernails? Because yesterday, during the battle, I noticed that some men—in fact, a *lot* of men—were having trouble opening their knives. Remember, you have to dig pretty hard to get the blade out. It's not like the magnifying glass.

Okay, another thing. Yesterday, on the battlefield, there was some confusion about the location of the blade. *If the logo is facing you, the blade is the third instrument on the right side of the knife.* It looks like the tweezers, but it's actually the one just above the tweezers. This is really important to remember.

Let's have a moment of silence to mourn all the men who died today.

Okay. One more thing: I can see that many of you have accidentally cut yourselves while trying to open your knives. Listen, this happens sometimes, it's just another part of war and army life. But try to be careful.

Tobias, how's the fire coming? Still sawing down the tree? Okay. Remember to be careful with that saw, Tobias. Just because it's little doesn't mean it isn't sharp.

All right, men, it looks like we have some more time before dinner. And as long as you're all here, I'd like to talk to you about respect. During weapons inspection, I noticed that many of you have lost your toothpicks. This is unacceptable. The toothpick is part of the Swiss Army knife. Yes, I know, it comes out. But that's not an excuse to lose it.

All right, that's it. Get some rest. Tomorrow we wage war.

how i imagine life in the u.s. army (based on the commercials i've seen)

GENERAL STONE: All right, men, listen up! Our nation is at war, and the whole world is counting on us to protect freedom. That leaves us with just one option.

BOB: Rock climbing?

GENERAL STONE: Exactly. There's a steep mountain in the middle of an unpopulated desert. We need someone to go there by himself, climb the mountain, and put a flag on the top.

BOB: I'll do it.

GENERAL STONE: Excellent! Here's the flag.

BOB: Cool.

GENERAL STONE: All right, let's see. We also need someone to ride a Jet Ski. How about you, Jackson?

JACKSON: I don't know, General, I'm sort of afraid of getting hurt. Can I stay here and work on computers?

GENERAL: Yes. Everybody who wants to can stay here and work on computers.

BRIAN: General?

GENERAL: What's up?

BRIAN: Can I take a break? I kind of want to go to college.

GENERAL: No problem, here's thirty thousand dollars in cash.

BRIAN: Great, thanks.

GENERAL: Okay, men, that's it for the day.

JACKSON: Hey, look! It's my friends and family.

FRIENDS AND FAMILY: Hey, nice uniform. We're proud of you.

JACKSON: Thanks. See you in a couple of weeks.

FRIENDS AND FAMILY: Yeah, see you then.

how did
all those fun army chants
get started?

—I don't know, but I've been told this next mission is suicide. Is it true?

—I don't know, John. But I've been told the same thing.

—I don't know. I've been told a mine exploded next to Brian's ear on the last mission.

—Sound off?

—Yep. He went deaf.

—One, two?

—Uh-huh. Both ears.

—Three, four?

—Four, Shawn. Four dead.

—I don't know, but I've been told we're not going home for a long time.

how college kids imagine the u.s. government

PRESENT DAY

—Did you hear the news, Mr. President? The students at the University of Pittsfield are walking out of their classes, in protest of the war.

—(Spits out coffee.) Wha—What did you say?

—Apparently, students are standing up in the middle of lectures and walking right out of the building.

—But students *love* lectures. If they're willing to give those up, they must really be serious about this peace thing! How did you hear about this protest?

—The White House hears about every protest, no matter how small.

—Oh, right, I remember.

—You haven't heard the half of it, Mr. President. The leader of the group says that if you don't stop the war today, they're going to . . . to . . . I'm sorry, I can't say it out loud. It's just too terrifying.

—Say it, dammit! I'm the President!

—All right! If you don't stop the war . . . they're going to stop going to school *for the remainder of the week.*

—Send the troops home.

—But, Mr. President! Shouldn't we talk about this?

—*Send the troops home.*

THE 60S

—Mr. President! Did you hear about Woodstock?

—Woo—Woodstock? What in God's name is that?

—Apparently, young people hate the war so much they're willing to participate in a musical sex festival in protest of it.

—Oh my God. They must really be serious about this whole thing.

—That's not all. Some of them are threatening to join communes: places where they make their own clothing . . . and beat on drums.

—Stop the war.

—But, Mr. President!

—Stop all American wars!

—(Sighs.) Very well, sir. I'll go tell the generals.

—Wow. It's a good thing those kids decided to go hear music.

war

LT. MCDOUGAL: Who among you will carry the flag as we march into battle?

ABBOT: I will!

LT. MCDOUGAL: And if this man goes down?

WALTER: Then I will hoist up the flag and carry it in his place!

LT. MCDOUGAL: And if this man goes down?

HAROLD: Then . . . I guess . . . I will carry the flag, sir!

LT. MCDOUGAL: And if this man goes down?

CHARLES: Then . . . well . . . I'll carry it.

LT. MCDOUGAL: And if this man goes down?

JOHN: Then . . . me? I guess? I'll carry it?

LT. MCDOUGAL: And if this man goes down?

WELLINGTON: Geez . . . I guess, then, I'll carry it. If it comes to that.

LT. MCDOUGAL: And if this man goes down?

MORTIMER: Sir . . . what kind of forces are we going up against? I mean . . . don't get me wrong, if Wellington takes a hit, I'll carry the flag—

LT. MCDOUGAL: And when this man goes down?

KEARNY: Sir? What do you think our chances are . . . of winning this battle? I'm not trying to get negative, I'm just . . . (Sighs.) Look, I'll carry the flag if he goes down. I'm just starting to get nervous—

LT. MCDOUGAL: And when this man goes down?

BILLINGS: Jesus. Captain, who are we fighting? What's the situation? Please, just be straight with us.

LT. MCDOUGAL: Who will carry the flag when Kearny goes down?

BILLINGS: Well, I guess me. I mean, I'd be the only one left . . . in that scenario.

LT. MCDOUGAL: All right. It goes Abbot, Walter, Harold, Charles, John, Wellington, Mortimer, Kearny, and then Billings. Forward march.

acknowledgments

I want to thank Daniel Greenberg and Dan Menaker for their advice, encouragement, and patience. I also want to thank my family, *The Harvard Lampoon,* Evan Camfield, Benjamin Dreyer, Stephanie Higgs, Jim Levine, and all the people who have gotten me out of desperate situations: Steve Bender, Kyle Berkman, Rob Dubbin, David Herson, Patrick Higgs, Azhar Kahn, Zach Kanin, Brent Katz, Farley Katz, Josh Koenigsberg, Jake Luce, Francesca Mari, Nick McDonnell, Josh Morgenthau, Andrei Nechita, Dan Selsam, Patrick Swieskowski, Nick Sylvester.

about the author

Simon Rich, a former president of *The Harvard Lampoon,*
will graduate from Harvard University in June 2007.